Now That You're a Christian

Bruce BICKEL
&
Stan JANTZ

HARVEST HOUSE PUBLISHERS

EUGENE, OREGON

CHRISTIANITY 101 is a registered trademark of Bruce Bickel and Stan Jantz. Harvest House Publishers, Inc., is the exclusive licensee of the federally registered trademark CHRISTIANITY 101.

Cover by Left Coast Design, Portland, Oregon

Cover illustration © Krieg Barrie Illustration

Bruce Bickel: Published in association with the literary agency of Mark Sweeney & Associates, 28540 Altessa Way, Ste. 201, Bonita Springs, FL 34135.

NOW THAT YOU'RE A CHRISTIAN
Copyright © 2005 by Bruce Bickel and Stan Jantz
Published by Harvest House Publishers
Eugene, Oregon 97402
www.harvesthousepublishers.com

ISBN 978-0-7369-2316-3

Printed in the United States of America

10 11 12 13 14 15 / BP-MS / 10 9 8 7 6 5

Contents

You've Made a Great Start...

You've made the choice to be a follower of Jesus Christ. That is an awesome decision, one that you will never regret. But we know that the initial stages of your new life as a Christian can be a bit intimidating. You may be thinking...

- What do I do next, and how do I learn more?
- Will my personality change?
- Am I expected to follow some rules and regulations?
- What have I gotten myself into?

We know that you might be vacillating between excitement, hesitation, and curiosity.

Well, you can start by taking a deep breath and relaxing. The process of growing as a Christian is as simple as getting to know someone who will become your best friend. In fact, it's easier than that because Jesus Christ is already in love with you, and He has been all along, even before you made the decision to follow Him.

The process of knowing God on an intimate, personal basis is not difficult. He wants that to happen. And as you learn more about Him, you'll realize how much He cares for you. What He said centuries ago still applies to you today:

> *"For I know the plans I have for you," says the LORD. "They are plans for good and not for disaster, to give you a future and a hope...when you pray, I will listen. If you look for me in earnest, you will find me when you seek me"* (Jeremiah 29:11-13).

What God Has Done for You

We know you are anxious to learn how this Christianity stuff affects you. But let's put *you* aside for a moment and focus instead on who *God* is. God is one God in three Persons—Father, Son, and Holy Spirit—who has made your salvation and your Christian life possible. By learning more about God, your appreciation of Him will deepen, and that's going to impact how you live your life and worship Him.

At a most basic level, Christianity simply involves a change in direction in our lives when we understand God's love for us. The apostle Paul said it this way to a group of people who, like you, were new in their Christian faith. Notice how each member of the Trinity—Father, Son, and Holy Spirit—is working in your life:

> *I pray that from [God's] glorious, unlimited resources he will give you mighty inner strength through his Holy Spirit. And I pray that Christ will be more and more at home in your hearts as you trust in him. May your roots go down deep into the soil of God's marvelous love. And may you have the power to understand, as all God's people should, how wide, how long, how high, and how deep his love really is. May you experience the love of Christ, though it is so great you will never fully understand it. Then you will be filled with the fullness of life and power that comes from God (Ephesians 3:16-19).*

Let's begin the process of understanding God's love by looking at what God the Father, God the Son, and God the Holy Spirit have done for you: God has saved you forever, Jesus has given you a new life, and the Holy Spirit has equipped you with a spiritual power source.

God Has Saved You Forever

The Bible reveals God's plan to establish a relationship with humanity. The Bible has lots of verses (a total of 31,101 to be exact), but we can quickly direct you to the one that sums it up succinctly:

> For God so loved the world that he gave his only Son, so that everyone who believes in him will not perish but have eternal life (John 3:16).

Let's dissect this verse to look at several of the components of salvation:

1. *"For God so loved the world..."* This is an incredible concept that is even more amazing than it might appear. Remember that God is perfect, and humanity is not. God is holy, and we are far from it. We aren't just a few notches below God on the righteousness scale; He is at the top, and we don't even make the chart. Yet God loves us in our "as is" condition. Despite all of our failings, flaws, and imperfections, He loves us.

2. *"...that he gave his only Son..."* We weren't pursuing Him; He initiated the steps to connect with us. Because our sins prevented the connection, the sacrifice of Christ on the cross was necessary to pay the penalty that we deserved.

3. *"...so that everyone who believes in him..."* Christianity is not limited to those of a particular country, political

group, ethnicity, or economic standing. It is available to everyone. The only criterion is *belief*. We have the choice to accept or reject God's offer of salvation. Our acceptance takes the form of believing that Christ's death and resurrection is the means by which our sins are forgiven and we establish a relationship with Christ. Belief is more than just intellectual acknowledgment of these facts; it includes intentionally choosing to follow God's plan rather than our own selfish desires.

4. *"...will not perish but have eternal life."* The physical death that awaits humanity is not the end; as spiritual beings with a soul, we have eternity before us. Christians will spend that eternity with Christ. But eternal life doesn't kick in only upon our death; it begins at the moment of our salvation.

The concepts that John 3:16 explains are examples of God's grace. *Grace* is a theological word that simply means "unmerited favor." God loves us, but we've done nothing to deserve His gift of salvation. Think about what God's grace means to you on a personal level:

- *God loves you unconditionally.* What you have done in the past doesn't matter. And because God already knows what you are going to do in the future, that doesn't matter either. His love doesn't hinge on what you've done or not done; it is unconditional because He is a God of grace.

- *God's salvation is a gift that none of us deserve.* This is a "come as you are" offer. You don't have to clean up your act to qualify. The offer isn't extended to you because you are good. Just the opposite. You aren't, and God knows you don't stand a chance of escaping hell without His gift of salvation. But don't ever think that just because salvation is free and readily available to you that it must be cheap. Always remember that your salvation came at the cost of Christ's own death on the cross.

- *You can do nothing to make God love you more*. Because God's love for you is already limitless, you don't have to worry about satisfying periodic performance testing to stay in His good graces. Oh, sure, you'll probably want to align your lifestyle to fall within His principles, but that will happen as you realize that God's blueprint for living makes sense. You are not under pressure to rack up brownie points with God; He wants your allegiance to Him to be motivated by love, not forced compliance.

- *You can do nothing to make God love you less*. Don't worry about God imposing some divine guilt trip on you. Sure, He desires that you live according to His principles. But God isn't going to love you less if you blow it from time to time. You won't be living under pressure to satisfy some angelic behavioral standard to retain your salvation. Doesn't that take some pressure off? Doesn't that make you more grateful for His grace?

In Bible terminology, *faith* and *belief* mean more than a confidence in certain circumstances (such as "I have faith in gravity" or "I believe gas prices will rise"). The kind of faith that leads to salvation involves your mind (belief), your spirit (trust), and your heart (adoration).

1. *Faith starts with belief*. Some skeptics of Christianity say it is only for the impressionable, the ignorant, the irrational, or the deluded. They say that faith requires the willful suspension of intellect. Nothing could be further from the truth. You are not saved by ignoring facts or truth. Just the opposite. Faith requires belief in (realization and appreciation of) the truth that Jesus is who He said He is, that the Bible is true, and that Christ is the way of salvation.

2. *Faith moves forward with trust.* *Trust* means that you have enough confidence in God to give Him ownership of your life. You are certain that His plan for you is better than your plan for yourself. And you are willing to build your life on that trust.

3. *Faith results in worship.* A sure sign of saving faith is the desire to worship God (to *worship* means to adore God, to give Him praise and reverent devotion, and to acknowledge His supremacy in all things). This type of worship rises naturally from an appreciation for the gift of salvation at the great cost of the sacrificial death of Jesus. A response of gratitude to God flows from true faith.

You exercised faith when you became a Christian, but the work of salvation was all on God's part. That means that the continuation of your salvation is not in jeopardy. If salvation were based on your constant compliance with a code of conduct, you'd lose out as soon as you slipped up. But since your salvation comes through God's grace and not by your performance, the gift of salvation is guaranteed forever. It's a done deal that won't be revoked. No one—not even you by your own screw-ups—can take away what Christ has paid for with His death. This is the concept of *eternal security,* and the Bible clearly states that nothing can invalidate your salvation:

> *And I am convinced that nothing can ever separate us from his love. Death can't, and life can't. The angels can't, and the demons can't. Our fears for today, our worries about tomorrow, and even the powers of hell can't keep God's love away...nothing in all creation will ever be able to separate us from the love of God that is revealed in Christ Jesus our Lord* (Romans 8:38-39).

Your New Life in Christ

Being called a Christian is no small thing. As a Christian, you are someone who has personally surrendered your life to Christ. You have accepted Jesus Christ as *Savior* and *Lord:*

- As your *Savior,* Jesus has literally saved you from eternal death and separation from God.
- As your *Lord,* Jesus now rules and reigns in your life.

We're going to look more carefully at what the saving life of Jesus and the lordship of Jesus really mean to you. But first, let's consider who Jesus is.

Who Is Jesus?

Have you ever wondered what God would look like? Is getting a mental picture of Him difficult for you? God knew that we mere mortals would have a difficult time conceptualizing a Spirit (that's what God is—see John 4:24), so He sent His only Son, Jesus, to be a tangible, visible presence of God on earth (See Colossians 1:15).

Jesus was God in human form. The word used to describe this is the *incarnation.* It literally means *taking* or *being flesh.* The Gospel of John says it this way:

> So the Word became human and lived here on earth among us (John 1:14).

We need to know two very important things about Jesus: He was fully human, and He was fully God.

—

- *Jesus was fully human.* Jesus had a human body, a mind, a soul, and emotions. He was so human that those who were closest to Him didn't think of Him as anything else. Yet even though He experienced all of our frailties, including temptation, Jesus never sinned. This gives us tremendous hope and comfort because we have a Savior who faced the same situations as we face, yet He never sinned (Hebrews 4:15-16).

- *Jesus was fully God.* The New Testament contains extensive proof for the deity of Christ. It uses the words *theos* (God) and *kyrios* (Lord) to refer to Christ. Jesus Himself made many claims to His deity (see John 8:58 and Revelation 22:13), and the New Testament writers also referred to Him as God (John 1:1). In addition, He provided ample physical evidence. Jesus had control over nature (Matthew 8:23-27), He forgave sins (Mark 2:1-12), and in the ultimate demonstration, He was resurrected after dying on the cross. This gives us tremendous assurance because our Savior can actually save us!

The incarnation is incredibly important because it's the Christian's answer to the question, how does God relate to the world? As Paul explained it, God had to become flesh so Jesus could save sinners by His perfect obedience and sinless life (Romans 5:18-19). Through the full humanity and the full deity of Jesus, God related to the world to bring us back into a right relationship with Him.

What Did Jesus Do?

Jesus became human in order to save us from our sins and make us right with God (Romans 3:22). Jesus accomplished this by dying on the cross. The crucifixion of Christ wasn't a tragedy. It was the divinely designed plan of God. Here is an abbreviated list of some of the basic accomplishments Christ achieved by His death on the cross. Each one is a vital part of God's plan of salvation for humankind:

—

1. *Substitution.* Christ died so that we don't have to. Every person who has ever lived is sinful (Romans 3:23), and the penalty for sin is eternal death (Romans 6:23). Jesus died in our place—He was our substitute—in order to satisfy God's righteous requirement (Romans 8:3-4).

2. *Propitiation.* Theologians use this word to explain that Christ's death on the cross turned God's wrath away from us. Because God is holy, He hates sin and is radically opposed to it. We are sinful beings, so that would make us the objects of God's wrath. But Christ's death on the cross appeased God's wrath (Romans 3:25).

3. *Redemption.* Before Christ died on the cross, we were slaves to sin. We were in bondage. Think of it as if Satan had kidnapped you and was holding you as a hostage. Your release depended on someone paying a ransom. That's exactly what Christ did on the cross. He paid the ransom to *redeem* you (literally, to purchase you back) from the slave market of sin. The ransom price was high. It cost Jesus His life (1 Peter 1:18-19).

4. *Reconciliation.* Humankind was alienated from God because of sin. Christ removed that alienation when He died on the cross. That made reconciliation between God and humanity possible (Romans 5:10-11).

Salvation comes from what Jesus did without any help from us. He did everything that was necessary. God requires nothing else of us but to accept what He did for us.

Where Is Jesus Now?

Jesus' death on the cross wasn't enough. In order to save us, Jesus had to come back to life. He had to be resurrected so that we could have eternal life (John 11:25-26). You can believe that the resurrection happened because it is a verifiable, historical event. In fact, you must believe in the resurrection to be saved (Romans 10:9). The death of Jesus removed the barrier between you and God, and the resurrection made your eternal life possible.

Jesus Is Lord

Forty days after His resurrection, Jesus ascended into heaven, where He is now in the place of honor next to God and where all the "angels and authorities and powers are bowing before him" (1 Peter 3:22). There, Jesus is engaged in at least three very important activities, all of which concern you:

- *Jesus is preparing a place for you.* You can be sure that Jesus is engaged in the most spectacular construction project in the history of the universe. He's preparing heaven... for you (John 14:2).

- *Jesus is praying for you.* Actually, the Bible says that Jesus is "pleading" to the Father on your behalf. Who better to plead your case before God? No one knows you better than Jesus (Hebrews 4:15-16).

- *Jesus is keeping the universe going for you.* The universe functions so beautifully for a reason: Jesus is holding all creation together (Colossians 1:17).

When you consider how much Jesus has done for you, and how much He continues to do for you right now, your response can only be to worship and praise Him as the Lord of your life. That was the apostle Paul's conclusion:

> *Because of this, God raised him up to the heights of heaven and gave him a name that is above every other name, so that at the name of Jesus every knee will bow, in heaven and on earth and under the earth, and every tongue will confess that Jesus Christ is Lord, to the glory of God the Father* (Philippians 2:9-11).

You Have an Inside Source

If you are like most new Christians, you're probably wishing you had some kind of guide or mentor to help explain the intricacies of Christianity. Actually, clarifying the intricacies would be a luxury that can wait; you probably feel that you've got more pressing and immediate needs:

- You want to please God, but how do you know what that entails?
- You want to read the Bible, but you aren't sure that you can make sense of it.
- You guess that you should be praying, but that puts you in unfamiliar territory.

Are you—a spiritual novice—unrealistic to think you can survive the Christian life without constant counseling by a spiritual advisor?

We've got good news and bad news for you in this regard. First, the bad news: Yes, you would be unrealistic to think that you can hack it as a Christian without intense guidance. But now for the good news: God has made arrangements for your personal spiritual tutor. And even better news: This spiritual mentor is not some seminary geek who is fluent in ancient Hebrew and has a complete set of disciple trading cards. Your personal spiritual counselor is none other than God Himself—in the Person of the Holy Spirit.

Don't get the wrong impression. The Holy Spirit is not just hovering around you like a chaperon at a high school prom.

The arrangement is much more intimate than that. The Holy Spirit actually lives inside each believer. Of course, the Holy Spirit won't show up on a CAT scan or in an X-ray, and you can't use Him as an excuse for that bloated feeling you've had recently. But if you are a follower of Christ, the Holy Spirit is present in your life.

Christians refer to this role of the Holy Spirit as His *indwelling*. Your body is like a temple for the Holy Spirit. That analogy isn't a stretch; it's in the Bible:

> *Or don't you know that your body is the temple of the Holy Spirit, who lives in you and was given by God?* (1 Corinthians 6:19).

When Jesus was on earth, He told His disciples that the Holy Spirit would be coming to indwell them and all other believers. Jesus described the Holy Spirit as a companion who would come alongside them to counsel, comfort, instruct, and advise them.

> *And I will ask the Father, and he will give you another Counselor, who will never leave you. He is the Holy Spirit, who leads into all truth* (John 14:16-17).

And that is just what the Holy Spirit will do for you:

1. *The Holy Spirit is a guarantee of your salvation.* As you learn to sense the Holy Spirit's presence in your life, He'll be the guarantee of your salvation. He is the proof that you belong to God.

2. *The Holy Spirit helps you know the mind of God.* The Holy Spirit can help you understand the Bible. He can give you spiritual insights that you could not comprehend on your own. Understanding the Word of God is the route to understanding the mind of God.

3. *The Holy Spirit helps you pray.* Prayer is an important part of the Christian life because it is how you will talk with God and tell Him your greatest needs and your deepest desires. It is how you will ask for direction. But how can you make sure that your prayers are getting past the ozone layer? That's where the Holy Spirit comes in. The Holy Spirit assists you in prayer. Even when you don't know what to say—or how to say it—the Holy Spirit can tell God what is in your heart. God will know exactly what you're feeling because the Holy Spirit is in complete harmony with God.

4. *The Holy Spirit helps you worship.* God deserves our praise and worship, but that isn't something that comes naturally to most of us, and we're awkward at it. The Holy Spirit will help you worship God in a way that pleases Him.

5. *The Holy Spirit helps you in your stress.* The Christian life is not easy. God never promised that it would be. But God has given the Holy Spirit to all believers to help them through the difficulties of life. Jesus referred to the Holy Spirit as our "Comforter," and that's exactly what He is.

6. *The Holy Spirit is your spiritual guide.* The Holy Spirit can lead and direct you in the circumstances and decisions of your life. This process isn't like using that Magic 8-Ball or picking a fortune cookie at random. It involves allowing the Holy Spirit to guide you step-by-step in daily situations, but this guidance will most often focus on your character and attitude rather than on innocuous choices, such as whether God wants you to wear the plaid shirt or the one with stripes.

7. *The Holy Spirit helps transform you.* The goal of every Christian is to be more like Christ. This will never happen completely in our lifetimes on earth, but the

Holy Spirit is engaged in the process of moving us in that direction.

8. *The Holy Spirit has a supernatural gift for you.* The Holy Spirit equips every Christian with a supernatural ability to minister. Although some of the spiritual gifts appear spectacular, most are more subtle. The spiritual sensitivity or results are what make these gifts supernatural.

With the indwelling of God's Holy Spirit, you've got the best counselor available for maturing in your Christian faith. It is a process that happens over time. We are confident you will make good progress. Every once in a while you will mess up (but the fault will be all yours, so don't try to blame it on poor parenting skills of your heavenly Father).

When some people's spiritual progress is particularly slow, they complain that they need to get more of the Holy Spirit into their life. They have it all wrong. Spiritual maturity is never a question of getting more of the Holy Spirit. If you are a believer, you already have all of Him. The question is just the opposite: "How much of *you* does the Holy Spirit have?" Spiritual growth is a matter of turning control of your life over to the Holy Spirit and following His direction instead of your own inclinations.

What God Wants You to Do

Now that you're a Christian, you probably want to know God's will for your life. It's only natural because now you are living for God and not for yourself. Even though people tend to worry about finding God's will, they don't have to—finding God's will isn't that difficult.

We're not talking about the specific things in your life—such as what kind of career you should pursue, whom you should marry, or where you should live. These are important matters (and they matter to God), but they aren't at the heart of what God wants you to do. In fact, living in the center of God's will for your life begins with God's work in your life:

> *We ask God to give you a complete understanding of what he wants to do in your lives, and we ask him to make you wise with spiritual wisdom. Then the way you live will always honor and please the Lord, and you will continually do good, kind things for others. All the while, you will learn to know God better and better* (Colossians 1:9-10).

Do you see how this works? God is ready to give you a complete understanding of what He wants to do in your life. He wants to make you wise. But God won't force Himself on you. It's up to you to please God by getting to know Him better and better. And the way to do that is to read and study His Word, learn how to talk with God through prayer, and regularly gather with other believers in church. If you do that, you're going to be in the center of God's will because you will be doing what He wants you to do.

Read the Bible

God wants you to read the Bible because that is the primary way God talks to you. Much more than a book, the Word of God is full of living power (Hebrews 4:12). When you realize that the Bible is God's personal message to you, you'll be anxious to read and study all that the Bible has to say. In this chapter we want to suggest that you approach your study of God's Word by learning how to properly interpret the Bible. But first you have to get the big picture.

The Big Picture

Even though the Bible is a collection of 66 separate books, it follows a basic chronological order. More impressive than that, it tells one basic story: *the relationship between God and people.* Once you understand the basic plot and where you are in the story line, everything you read will make sense. Here is how the story of the great drama of the relationship between God and humanity is laid out:

1. *God created a perfect fellowship.* The first two chapters of the Bible describe how God created Adam and Eve and how the three of them had a great friendship going. Everything was perfect in the Garden of Eden. This part of the God/human drama takes only 56 verses to tell because, unfortunately, it didn't last very long.

2. *People broke the relationship.* People sinned (which is falling short of God's perfect standard), breaking the relationship between God and humanity. The rest of the Old Testament and the first four books of the New Testament

describe the details of God's plan to restore the relationship. Here are some highlights of this part of the Bible:

- *Sin has consequences.* Adam and Eve exercised their own free will and chose to follow their desires instead of God's instructions. Their disobedience plunged the entire human race into misery and separation from God, resulting in God's judgment against sin.

- *God chooses a people and lays down the Law.* God wanted to show the world that people who follow His laws receive His blessings. He selected the descendants of Abraham (later called the Israelites or Jews) to be His chosen people for this purpose. God also planned to bring Jesus into the world through Abraham's bloodline (see Genesis 12:3 and Matthew 1:1). God gave the Ten Commandments to show the behavior that He finds acceptable. As illustrated throughout the Old Testament, no one is able to keep all of the commandments and live up to God's perfect standard.

- *A nation finds a place to call home.* God led the nation of Israel into the promised land after a time of slavery in Egypt and 40 years of wilderness training. But life was a constant battle (literally) because God's people continued to disobey God's explicit directives. The people rejected God as their king and demanded a human king. Eventually Israel's adversaries invaded them and forced them into exile. Little by little the Jews were able to return to their homeland and rebuild the city of Jerusalem.

- *The cry of the prophets.* God used prophets (a prophet is one who speaks for God) to warn the people of the consequences of their disobedience and to implore them to turn back to God. Some of these prophets lived while Israel was in its homeland, and others spoke during the times of exile.

- *The promised Messiah arrives.* A 400-year gap separates the Old and New Testaments. The Jews were back in their homeland, waiting for the Messiah. God had promised to Abraham that reconciliation would establish a new kingdom on earth.

3. *God can restore the relationship.* The only way God could restore His relationship with humanity was to solve the sin problem.

- *Jesus paid the penalty.* The death of Jesus paid the penalty for humanity's sin. It is the focal point of the entire Bible because it is the seminal event for reconciling humankind to God. Each of the four Gospels tells the story of the death and resurrection of Christ.

- *Maturing is a process.* In the first century, missionaries such as the apostle Paul established churches, which were places where Christians met together to worship God, listen to teaching, and fellowship with one another. Some of the disciples of Jesus (a disciple is a learner) wrote letters to these churches to explain concepts about accepting Christ as Savior and then growing in a deeper relationship with Him.

- *We'll be reunited at the end.* The Bible ends appropriately with a look into the future. The book of Revelation describes the events that will mark the end of the world (as we know it), including the second coming of Jesus Christ and the establishment of God's eternal kingdom, where Christians will live with Him forever.

How to Interpret the Bible

As you read and study the Bible, the most important thing you can do is to bring out the meaning. This is known as *interpretation.* When you interpret something, you make it plain and understandable. Here are some basic principles of interpretation:

1. *Context rules.* Whenever you read a chapter, a verse, or

even a word of Scripture, it must always be taken in *context,* which means "that which goes with the text."

2. *Scripture will never contradict Scripture.* If two passages of Scripture seem to be in contradiction, one of two things is going on. Either your interpretation is wrong, or your understanding is limited.

3. *Interpret Scripture literally.* This means you interpret the Bible *as it is written.* As you read the Bible, consider the literary form or style, such as poetry, prophecy, and historical narrative.

4. *Look for the author's intended meaning.* Don't read something into a verse or passage that isn't there, and don't skip over something that is. Let the passage speak for itself.

5. *Check your conclusions by using reliable Bible commentaries.* Regardless of how knowledgeable you are, a good commentary (or a good Bible teacher) can be a plumb line for your own understanding and interpretation.

6. *Live in the power of the Holy Spirit.* One of the most important things the Holy Spirit does is to help you understand God's Word (John 14:16-17). The Holy Spirit is your inside source, helping you to understand the things of God as you study the Bible.

Study the Bible for Life

With all this talk about study and effort, you could conclude that studying the Bible is like taking a course in school (only without the grade). But it's much more than that. At its best, Bible study is a life-changing process that will result in God's blessing—but only if you apply what the Bible says to your life (see James 1:22-25).

Do you want God to bless you? Do you want to live a life filled with God's transforming power? Then study the Bible, learn to interpret it correctly, and apply what it says to your life. This is what God wants you to do (2 Timothy 3:16-17).

Learn to Pray

Before you start worrying about *what to say* when you pray, let's consider whether you should pray at all. You've got many other things to think about as a new Christian. Perhaps this seemingly super-spiritual practice of prayer is more appropriate for the veteran Christians than for the rookies.

Apparently not. God makes very clear that He wants all Christians to be praying because this is the primary way you talk with God. The Bible is pretty blunt about it, with verses like these:

> *Pray at all times* (Ephesians 6:18).
>
> *Devote yourselves to prayer* (Colossians 4:2).
>
> *Keep on praying* (1 Thessalonians 5:17).

God doesn't ask us to pray because He is lonesome. (Don't flatter yourself. He's not lonely, and you're not that great of a conversationalist.) God wants you praying because prayer gets Him involved in your life. His involvement is essential if you are going to grow as a Christian. Consider these examples:

- You gain spiritual strength through prayer.
- You are equipped to resist temptation through prayer.
- God will give you wisdom if you pray for it.
- Prayer plays a part in physical healing.
- You'll only get to know God better as you communicate with Him.

Most importantly, prayer brings you into God's presence. Conversing with God takes you out of your humdrum world and connects you with the Creator of the universe. And that happens immediately. God doesn't have a waiting room where you have to sit for 35 minutes before talking with Him. He doesn't put you on hold and force you to listen to angelic harp-plucking while He answers prayers in the order that they are received. Nope. When you pray, you are immediately in God's presence, and you've got His undivided attention.

Immature Christians (notice that we didn't say "new" Christians) often make the mistake of treating prayer like rubbing a genie's lamp—they only do it when they want to get something. Prayer isn't about getting stuff. Yes, many benefits can come to you through prayer, but at its core, the purpose of prayer is to connect you to God.

Let's admit it. We all tend to be self-centered, and that perspective can spill over into our prayers. But don't let that happen. You should expect prayer to change your attitude and focus. Our prayers should properly focus on who God is and what He wants to accomplish in our lives. As you pray sincerely, you will begin to align yourself with God's plans rather than your own. This approach will help you subordinate what you want to His desires. As you pray, you make God the focal point of your life. You'll change from being self-centered to being God-centered.

Another key to praying is to be yourself. After all, God knows who you are (and already loves you), so you don't need to pretend to be different from who you really are. When you talk with a friend, the most effective means of communication is talking face-to-face in normal, everyday language with no pretense, no hidden agendas, and no false formality. The same goes for communicating with God. Even though you can't see Him, you can talk to Him in person because you are always in His presence. Just be yourself.

God has been listening to prayers for thousands of years.

During that time, people have been praying in a lot of different languages and a lot of different styles. They have prayed while they were mad, happy, scared, and thoughtful. God wants you to pray the way you feel. Be honest with Him. Don't get hung up over things like these:

- *The way you speak:* You can pray silently in your mind, or you can talk to God out loud.
- *Your body language:* You can be standing, sitting, kneeling, or lying down.
- *What you do with your hands:* They can be folded, raised, or in your pockets.
- *Your eyes:* They can be open or closed.

We're sure you get the point here. Prayer has no right or wrong posture. God is more interested in the attitude of your heart than the position of your body.

The prospect of praying might be intimidating if you're worried about what to say. That shouldn't be a problem; God just wants you to talk with Him about those things that are of concern to you. But just in case you're still drawing a blank, here are a few suggestions:

1. *Praise God for who He is.* This is more for you than for Him. Praise reminds you that no one in heaven or on earth can compare with Him. You'll be impressed with the fact that conversing with God is an awesome privilege.

2. *Confess your sins.* God forgave your sins (past, present, and future) when you accepted Christ as your Savior. Sin in your life from this point on won't jeopardize your salvation, but it will interfere with your ability to communicate openly and honestly with God. Without confession and an apology on your part, you'll be living in spiritual arrogance. Let God know that you are sorry for your sins, and get your relationship back on track.

3. *Pray for God's will.* You'll have your own ideas about what should happen in your life, but tell God that you want what He knows is best for you (even if it is different from what you have in mind).

4. *Pray for others.* It's not all about you. Pray for others who are in difficult situations. Pray that they might see their need for Jesus. If they are already Christians, pray that they might feel His comfort and sense His wisdom.

Sometimes you will be distraught or confused and won't even be able to articulate words. In those situations, don't worry. The Holy Spirit can communicate with God for you when you are speechless:

> *And the Holy Spirit helps us in our distress. For we don't even know what we should pray for, nor how we should pray. But the Holy Spirit prays for us with groanings that cannot be expressed in words. And the Father who knows all hearts knows what the Spirit is saying, for the Spirit pleads for us believers in harmony with God's own will* (Romans 8:26-27).

Notice that we have been referring to prayer as talking *with* God—not talking *to* Him. Prayer is a two-way conversation. You will do some of the talking while God listens. But then you need to let God do some of the talking while you listen. When we refer to letting God talk, we don't expect that you will be hearing little angel voices in your head. We don't even think that you will hear God using His best James Earl Jones impression with a deep bass voice booming down from heaven.

God is most likely to speak to you in the quietness of your thoughts. As you pray for His direction, you are going to get a sense of what He wants. He will speak to you by prompting your thoughts.

Go to Church

Next to reading the Bible and praying, the most important thing you can do in your Christian life is go to church. That's because the church is not some human idea or invention. The church is God's great idea. Church is where the people who "belong to the Lord" and who have been "called out" by God (that's what the word *church* literally means) gather regularly to worship God, study the Bible, and encourage one another.

Even though you probably go to a specific church, the definition of *church* is much broader than a particular location. In reality, the church includes all Christians—those who believe in the God of the Bible and have received Jesus Christ as their personal Savior—for all time. In other words, all Christians living today are part of the church, but so are all believers who have died. Here are some other qualities of the church:

- *The church is invisible and visible.* The church includes all genuine believers for all time, so in one sense, the church is *invisible.* From our human perspective, we don't know for sure who the true believers are, even in the church we attend. That's because we can't see people the way God sees them (2 Timothy 2:19). At the same time, the church is definitely *visible.* Professing Christians are the visible representation of the church.

- *The church is local and universal.* The word *church* can apply to local groups, and it can also apply to the universal church, which is the church throughout the world. The bottom line is that all those who have been called out by God at any level are part of the church.

Metaphors for the Church

To help us understand the true nature of the church, the Bible gives us several helpful metaphors and images. Here are three that relate to the three persons of the Trinity:

- *The people of God.* In the history of salvation, God has always called out people for Himself, for His purpose, and for His glory. The church is also called the "family" of God. God is our heavenly Father (Ephesians 3:14), and we are His sons and daughters (2 Corinthians 6:18).

- *The body of Christ.* This is the apostle Paul's favorite metaphor for the church, and he uses it in two ways. First, the body of Christ is the church as a body with various parts or members that function together for service. This part of the metaphor emphasizes the *diversity* and *mutuality* of the church. We all have different gifts, and we all need each other (1 Corinthians 12:12-27). The other way Paul uses the metaphor emphasizes the *unity* of the church. We are all one body, and Christ is the head (Ephesians 1:22-23; 4:15-16).

- *The temple of the Holy Spirit.* A temple is a physical place where God dwells. The church is like that because it is the place where God dwells with His people through the Holy Spirit. He lives in each of us individually (1 Corinthians 6:19) and in the church corporately (1 Corinthians 3:16).

What to Expect When You Go to Church

If you've been going to church for a while, then none of what we're about to share with you will be a surprise. But if you're new to this church business, then you may find some helpful information about what to expect when you go to church.

1. *You will be worshiping God.* Music, praise, and worship

have always been vital parts of the Christian church experience. The apostle Paul says that songs and praises are natural responses of a person who is filled with the Holy Spirit (Ephesians 5:18-19). Worship styles will vary from traditional to contemporary. There is no right or wrong way to worship God as long as you are directing praise to Him.

2. *You will be hearing the Word.* When you were saved, the Word of God played an important part. Now that you're a Christian, the Word of God is able to "build you up" (Acts 20:32). That's why going to a church where the Bible is taught consistently and systematically is so important.

3. *You will be participating in Communion.* The early church met together to participate in the Lord's Supper (Acts 2:44-47), and today's church is no different. When you go to church, you will celebrate the Lord's Supper, also known as Communion. By using the symbolism of bread and wine, the act of Communion commemorates the fact that Christ died for our sins (see 1 Corinthians 11:23-26). The remembrance is what is important, not the way Communion is administered.

4. *You will be participating in baptism.* Jesus wants His followers to be baptized, not because it's required for salvation but because baptism is the way you make a public profession of your new life in Christ. Jesus placed an emphasis on baptism in His Great Commission (Matthew 28:18-20), so it must be pretty important. Whenever baptism appears in the Bible, someone is immersed in the water. This contains some good symbolism: When we accept Christ as Savior, our old nature dies (the "going under the water" part), and we become a new creature in Christ (the "coming out of the water" part). Not all churches baptize by immersion—some

prefer to "sprinkle"—which shows us once again that the logistics of baptism aren't as important as the statement you make by doing it.

5. *You will be giving your tithes and offerings.* The Bible has a lot to say about money. God doesn't need your money, but you need to give your money as He directs. God wants you to honor Him with your finances, and He wants you to be a trustworthy steward (manager) of all the resources He has given to you. All of your resources belong to Him, and you should be using them for His glory.

6. *You will be putting your spiritual gifts to work.* Your involvement in a local church is essential to your growing life in Christ because that will be the place where you will discover, exercise, and develop your spiritual gifts. As a Christian, you have at least one spiritual gift, which is given to you by the Holy Spirit for the purpose of helping and serving others (1 Corinthians 12:7). You will find lists of spiritual gifts in 1 Corinthians 12:4-11; Romans 12:6-8; and 1 Peter 4:10-11.

Which Church Is the Best?

First of all, if you're looking for the best or the perfect church, you're going to be disappointed because churches contain imperfect people! Rather than looking for the perfect church, get involved with a growing church where people worship God, teach the Word, practice Communion and baptism, and where you have the opportunity to use your spiritual gifts.

Having God's Heart

Your success at walking in the Christian life will depend upon a continuing and deepening relationship with Jesus Christ. You must stay connected with Him. Jesus explained this relationship to His disciples this way:

> *Remain in me, and I will remain in you. For a branch cannot produce fruit if it is severed from the vine, and you cannot be fruitful apart from me. Yes, I am the vine; you are the branches. Those who remain in me, and I in them, will produce much fruit. For apart from me you can do nothing* (John 15:4-5).

Staying connected with Christ is not solely for your benefit. Yes, it will change you from the inside out, and you'll be a better person. But your relationship with Christ provides a collateral benefit to others. Just as Jesus had compassion for you, as you become more like Him, you'll find that you have more love and compassion for others.

Remember that as a Christian, you carry the name of Christ with you wherever you go. In a sense, you are an ambassador for Jesus:

> *And whatever you do or say, let it be as a representative of the Lord Jesus* (Colossians 3:17).

As much for others as for yourself, you need to reflect the love of Christ. Bring His character into your relationships. Reflect His love to those you know. And don't hesitate to share the change that is happening in your life now that you've become a Christian.

Loving One Another

What is the best way to convince people that following Christ can transform their life? Is it more effective to tell them or to show them? The correct answer is to show them, but it is also the more difficult approach. Anyone can say that Christianity makes you different; proving the point by your lifestyle is an entirely different matter.

Jesus knew human nature (that we are basically self-centered beings). And He knew that Christians could make the greatest impression on people around them by behaving in a manner that was counterintuitive. That's why He wants Christians to show love to each other. Here is His explanation to His disciples:

> *So now I am giving you a new commandment: Love each other. Just as I have loved you, you should love each other. Your love for one another will prove to the world that you are my disciples* (John 13:34-35).

Notice that this wasn't just a helpful suggestion. Christ gave this as a commandment. He wants us to be involved in the lives of other Christians. He knows that the members of the Christian community need to support each other. And their commitment to each other will be the best reflection of the character of Christ to the unbelieving world.

From a practical standpoint, what does this "love one another" in the Christian community look like? That's a good question, and some new Christians in the first century must have had the same question. Here is how the apostle Paul explained it to them:

> *Since God chose you to be the holy people whom he loves, you must clothe yourselves with tenderhearted mercy, kindness, humility, gentleness, and patience. You must make allowance for each other's faults and forgive the person who offends you. Remember, the Lord forgave you, so you must forgive others. And the most important piece of clothing you must wear is love. Love is what binds us all together in perfect harmony. And let the peace that comes from Christ rule in your hearts. For as members of one body you are all called to live in peace. And always be thankful* (Colossians 3:12-15).

Don't misunderstand the emphasis. Yes, Jesus wants you to love other Christians, but that directive doesn't sanction rude and crude behavior toward non-Christians. Love is a trademark of Christ, and He extended His love to the entire world (remember John 3:16?). So your new life should be marked by care and compassion for all people. Here is how Jesus explained it when someone asked Him which commandment was the most important:

> *You must love the Lord your God with all your heart, all your soul, and all your mind. This is the first and greatest commandment. A second is equally important: Love your neighbor as yourself* (Matthew 22:37-39).

We know what you may be thinking: Loving other Christians may be difficult enough, but showing love to everyone is impossible. We agree with you. It is not humanly possible. But you are still capable of doing it—not in your own strength but through the supernatural power of the Holy Spirit.

As you get to know Christ better, and as you learn to let the Holy Spirit influence you, your life will begin to reflect God's character. The Bible refers to the character qualities that God possesses—and that the Holy Spirit imparts to us—as "fruit of the Spirit."

> *But when the Holy Spirit controls our lives, he will produce this kind of fruit in us: love, joy, peace, patience, kindness, goodness, faithfulness, gentleness, and self-control* (Galatians 5:22-23).

Consider how this "fruit" (if it is present in your life) will enable you to fulfill Christ's commandment to love other Christians and anyone else that you know or meet:

- *Love*—We should model our love after God, who Himself is love. We should love with the same sacrificial love that motivated God to send Jesus into the world.

- *Joy*—The world strives for happiness, but Christians should seek joy. The difference is that happiness depends on outward circumstances, but joy is based on obeying Jesus and knowing that He loves us. Happiness is transitory; joy is permanent. People will notice the difference in your life.

- *Peace*—Friction exists between people and nations. Peace among people is temporary. But God's peace is lasting. You will be able to display the peace of God "which is far more wonderful than the human mind can understand" (Philippians 4:7). People will be curious about your faith if you exhibit peace during difficult circumstances.

- *Patience*—In a society that demands instant gratification, your patience will be noticeable. Wait for God's timing in the situations of your life without complaining or fretting. The world will want to know your secret.

- *Kindness*—Nothing is random about a spiritual act of kindness. It may be spontaneous, but it is the deliberate act of treating others fairly even if they treat you harshly. Having this attitude means treating them the way God does.

- *Goodness*—This involves helping people, not because they deserve it but because you want to. It reflects a heart of generosity.

- *Faithfulness*—To be faithful means that you are "entirely trustworthy and good" (Titus 2:10). If you are faithful, you are a person of your word and a person of God's Word.

- *Gentleness*—Nothing is wimpy about someone who displays the character trait of gentleness. Think of a wild horse that has been tamed. The power is still there, but it is under control. Christians should be gentle people who have the confidence of knowing they have God's power.

- *Self-Control*—This is the ability to have mastery over your thoughts and actions. If you have spiritual self-control, you let the Holy Spirit control your life. To keep your natural desires in check, you need to make a choice every day and in every way to "live according to your new life in the Holy Spirit" (Galatians 5:16).

Are you incapable of consistently reflecting those character traits? Maybe not, but as the Holy Spirit works in your life, they'll be more and more noticeable in your life. This is the kind of "fruit" that reflects the heart of God to the world around you. And that's the reason for it all. Remember what Jesus said:

> *My true disciples produce much fruit. This brings great glory to my Father* (John 15:8).

Becoming a Disciple

The New Testament uses the word *disciple* to describe the relationship between Jesus and His followers. People often referred to Jesus as *Rabbi* (which means teacher), and they called anyone who followed Him a *disciple* (which means learner). A disciple was anyone who believed in Jesus (John 8:31) and who learned from Him (Matthew 5:1). The same is true today. A disciple of Jesus is one who has trusted Jesus as Savior and Lord and who desires to learn from Him and follow Him fully.

Become a Disciple

Jesus is the one who calls us to be His disciples (Matthew 4:19). And He doesn't just ask us to learn from Him. Jesus wants us to follow Him in everything we do. Discipleship means that we commit to the *Person* of Christ as well as the *teachings* of Christ.

- *Commit to the Person of Christ.* When you commit yourself to someone, you do everything you can to please that person. You carry out their wishes. In other words, you obey them. In our culture, obedience can have a negative connotation because it means submitting to someone else. But when it comes to committing ourselves to Christ, isn't that exactly what we need to do? To commit ourselves to the Person of Christ means that we submit to Him and obey Him. Obedience is the way we show God that we're serious about following Him and doing what He wants.

- *Commit to the teachings of Christ.* Jesus was the greatest teacher who ever lived, but He was more than a great teacher. Jesus was God in human form, who came to earth to tell and to show us how to live. A disciple of Jesus learns from Jesus by reading and studying God's Word. That's because the Bible points to Jesus (John 5:39). Beginning in Genesis and continuing throughout the Scriptures, the Bible points to Jesus. As you read and study the Bible, keep in mind that your discipleship is based on what you *are* to Jesus, not what you *do* for Him. A disciple is not one who checks off a list of what he or she has done for Jesus. A disciple is one who is devoted to Jesus.

Make Disciples

Being a disciple of Jesus is not enough. You must also make disciples of others. That's the last thing Jesus said just before He left the earth and ascended into heaven:

> *Jesus came and told his disciples, "I have been given complete authority in heaven and on earth. Therefore, go and make disciples of all the nations, baptizing them in the name of the Father and the Son and the Holy Spirit. Teach these new disciples to obey all the commands I have given you. And be sure of this: I am with you always, even to the end of the age"* (Matthew 28:18-20).

Our obedience to this command of Christ is imperative. Notice that the command has three parts:

1. *Make disciples.* The way to do this is to share your faith (we'll talk more about this in the next chapter) through the power of Scripture and the Holy Spirit so that others will turn from their sin to Christ and follow Him as their

Savior and Lord. Notice that we are not expected to *save* others. That's what God does. Our job is to disciple them.

2. *Baptize them.* This doesn't mean that we are the ones doing the baptizing. What this means is that at some point the new believer should "go public" and declare to other believers and the world that he or she intends to follow Jesus. It also means that the new believer is part of the body of Christ (1 Corinthians 12:13). The true disciple of Jesus will want to join other disciples in a local church.

3. *Teach them.* Helping new believers get established in their faith is vitally important. As you know, new Christians are vulnerable to doubt, fear, and temptation. Overcoming these negatives in isolation is almost impossible. A new believer needs nurturing, encouragement, and teaching. As you grow in your own Christian life, Jesus expects—no, He *commands* you to help new believers grow in their faith. Remember, maturing in Christ takes time. Disciples must have devoted and patient teachers who will stick with them through thick and thin.

As you obey the Lord in these areas, notice that Jesus has given you the means to carry out this command. First, all authority has been given to Jesus, so what He says is the absolute truth. Second, Jesus promises to be with you to the end of the age. This is a huge promise that should give you great comfort and encouragement as you follow and obey Him as His disciple.

Sharing Your Faith

Immediately before Jesus left earth and ascended into heaven, He gave this final instruction to His followers:

> *But when the Holy Spirit has come upon you, you will receive power and will tell people about me everywhere* (Acts 1:8).

Jesus said that we are supposed to be His witnesses. That means we should tell people what we know about Him. Plain and simple.

Sharing your faith should be the most natural thing in the world because it's really nothing more than telling someone else the story of what God has done for you personally. It doesn't have to be in a fancy speech or in a well-crafted presentation; in fact, it is usually better if it isn't. The essence of Christianity is a relationship with Jesus, so you're better off by simply sharing your personal story of what Christ means to you (it is called your "testimony").

You might be reluctant to share your faith because you don't know how people will respond. *Will I be ridiculed? Might I offend someone?* Don't worry about it. Nothing is objectionable about someone sharing about his or her spiritual journey in a sincere and respectful manner.

Try to remember that sharing your faith isn't really about you. And it's not even about getting a yes or no answer from the person you're talking to. It's all about God and simply talking about His incredible gift of salvation. This means that you are relieved of a lot of pressure:

- *You aren't supposed to be Jesus' public relations agent.* He doesn't need you to build up a bunch of hype about Him. Don't alter what you have to say based on what you think your friends want to hear. Just tell them about Jesus as you know Him.

- *You aren't His sales force.* You aren't paid on a commission based on how many people you get to sign a "salvation" contract. You shouldn't use pressure tactics. You aren't trying to "make a sale."

- *He doesn't need a marketing strategist.* Don't think that you need to trick people into learning about Jesus. Be upfront and straightforward with people. Jesus can take it from there.

People don't need a religion, but they do need Jesus. Don't get distracted from this simple message: Jesus loves them, He died on a cross to pay the penalty for their sins, and He wants to establish a personal relationship with them.

Don't worry about answering every conceivable theological question. You only need to talk about what you have found to be true in your own experience. No one can honestly expect you to have all of the answers (especially since many mysteries about God have existed for thousands of years).

Leave the sermons to the pastors. Your friends and family don't want to hear any preaching from you. They don't need to be lectured, scolded, or ridiculed. You are not properly representing Jesus if you are alienating these people when you present God's message to them. Sure, they are sinners, but so are you. Jesus hates your sin, but He loves you. And you should show that same love to all of the unsaved people you know.

Sharing your faith effectively—through your character, your

conduct, and your words—is simply the natural outgrowth of loving God.

- As you love God more, you will be more excited about the things He is doing in your life. Your excitement about God will make talking to other people about Him easier.

- As you love God more, your understanding of Him will grow. Your relationship with Him will become even more personal. Then explaining your relationship with God to those who don't know Him will be even easier for you.

- As you love God more, you won't have to force yourself to share your faith. You will be doing it naturally—your deeds and words will be a testimony of God's love— because the Holy Spirit is producing God's character in your life.

Once people know you are a Christian, they will be examining your life to see if your faith is legitimate. Oh sure, we want our unsaved family and friends to be paying attention to us when we are acting spiritual. But we don't want them watching when...

- we yell a few colorful comments at the referee who makes a bad call,

- we're laughing at a crude and offensive joke,

- a driver cuts us off on the freeway and we slander his intelligence or lineage, or

- we're gossiping about the people we work with.

Effective witnessing involves a combination of your character, your conduct, and your communication. All of these aspects of your life should be reflections of Jesus Christ. This is what sharing your faith is all about—telling and showing other people what Jesus is like. You can *tell* them by what you *say*, but you will *show* them by what you *do*.

More to Help You Grow

You'll grow in your faith as you get to know Jesus better. You can start by reading a little bit about Him each day. Here is a 30-day reading plan that will get you started:

1. God became a human being . . . . *John 1:1-18*
2. An angel promises Mary the birth of Jesus . . . . *Luke 1:26-38*
3. Jesus is born in Bethlehem . . . . *Luke 2:1-7*
4. John baptizes Jesus . . . . *Matthew 3:13-17*
5. Nicodemus visits Jesus at night . . . . *John 3:1-21*
6. Jesus talks to a woman at the well . . . . *John 4:1-26*
7. Jesus provides a miraculous cath of fish . . . . *Luke 5:1-11*
8. Jesus claims to be God's Son . . . . *John 5:19-30*
9. Jesus gives the Beatitudes . . . . *Matthew 5:1-12*
10. Jesus teaches about worry . . . . *Matthew 6:25-34*
11. Jesus forgives an adulterous woman . . . . *John 7:53-8:11*
12. Jesus comforts Mary and Martha . . . . *John 11:17-37*
13. Jesus rides into Jerusalem on a donkey . . . . . . *John 12:12-19*
14. Jesus tells about the future . . . . *Matthew 24:1-25*
15. Jesus prays for himself . . . . *John 17:1-5*
16. Jesus prays for his disciples . . . . *John 17:6-19*
17. Jesus agonizes in the garden . . . . *Mark 14:32-42*
18. Caiaphas questions Jesus . . . . *Mark 14:53-65*
19. Jesus stands trial before Pilate . . . . *Matthew 27:11-14*
20. Pilate hands Jesus over to be crucified . . . . . . *Mark 15:6-15*
21. Jesus is led away to be crucified . . . . *Mark 15:21-24*
22. Jesus is placed on the cross . . . . *Mark 15:25-32*
23. Jesus dies on the cross . . . . *Mark 15:33-41*
24. Jesus is laid in the tomb . . . . *Mark 15:42-47*
25. Jesus rises from the dead . . . . *Matthew 28:1-7*
26. Jesus appears to the women . . . . *Matthew 28:8-10*
27. Jesus appears to the disciples . . . . *John 20:24-31*
28. Jesus talks with Peter . . . . *John 21:15-25*
29. Jesus gives the great commission . . . . *Matthew 28:16-20*
30. Jesus ascends into heaven . . . . *Luke 24:50-53*

Christianity 101® Series

Now That You're a Christian

If you're a new believer, you'll connect with these honest, encouraging responses to questions that new Christians often have. You'll discover what God has done for humanity, how you can know Him better, and how you can reflect the love of Christ to people around you.

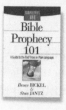

Bible Prophecy 101

In their contemporary, down-to-earth way, Bruce and Stan present the Bible's answers to your end-times questions. You will appreciate their helpful explanations of the rapture, the tribulation, the millennium, Christ's second coming, and other important topics.

Creation & Evolution 101

In their distinctive, easy-to-access style, Bruce and Stan explore the essentials of creation and evolution and offer fascinating evidence of God's hand at work. Perfect for individual or group use.

Knowing the Bible 101

Enrich your interaction with Scripture with this user-friendly guide, which shows you the Bible's story line and how each book fits into the whole. Learn about the Bible's themes, terms, and culture, and find out how you can apply the truths of every book of the Bible to your own life.

Knowing God 101

Whatever your background, you will be inspired by these helpful descriptions of God's nature, personality, and activities. You will also find straightforward responses to the essential questions about God.

Bible Answers 101

Using hundreds of questions from readers, Bruce and Stan tackle some of the biggest issues about life and living the Christian faith, including, *What happens when we die? Is Christ the only way to salvation? How can we know there is a God? Is the Bible true?*

Growing as a Christian 101

In this fresh look at the essentials of the Christian walk, Bruce and Stan offer you the encouragement you need to continue making steady progress in your spiritual life.

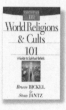

World Religions and Cults 101

This study features key teachings of each religion, quick-glance belief charts, biographies of leaders, and study questions. You will discover the characteristics of cults and how each religion compares to Christianity.

Evidence for Faith 101

Bruce and Stan present Christian apologetics without polemics and without clichés as they tackle vital questions people of all ages and beliefs are asking. Examine evidence— from history, from the lives of people changed by faith, and from our world—as you form and under- stand your convictions about God.

Christianity 101® Bible Studies

Genesis: Discovering God's Answers to Life's Ultimate Questions

"In the beginning" says it all. Genesis sets the stage for the drama of human history. This guide gives you a good start and makes sure you don't get lost along the way.

Galatians: Walking in God's Grace

With their trademark humor, deep respect for the authority of Scripture, and penetrating insights into current trends, Bruce and Stan reveal the serious problems Paul addressed and practical solutions he provided. They show that his presentation of God's grace speaks as forcefully today as it did to his original readers.

John: Encountering Christ in a Life-Changing Way

This study reveals who Jesus is by demonstrating the dramatic changes He made in the lives of the people He met, including Nicodemus, the woman at the well, Lazarus, and John, "the disciple whom Jesus loved."

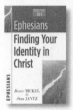

Ephesians: Finding Your Identity in Christ

Verse for verse, the book of Ephesians is one of the most profound, powerful, and practical books in the Bible. This guide reveals the heart of Paul's teaching on who believers are in Christ.

Acts: Living in the Power of the Holy Spirit

Bruce and Stan offer a straightforward look at the ongoing ministry of Jesus through the church. They highlight the drama of the early Christians' triumph over darkness and their explosive growth from a band of 120 fearful followers to a thriving, worldwide church.

Philippians/Colossians: Experiencing the Joy of Knowing Christ

This new 13-week study of two of Paul's most intimate letters will inspire you to know Christ more intimately and maintain your passion and vision. Filled with helpful background information, up-to-date applications, and penetrating, open-ended questions.

Romans: Understanding God's Grace and Power

Paul's letter to the church in Rome is his clearest explanation and application of the good news. This fresh study of Romans assures you that the Gospel is God's answer to every human need.

James: Working Out Your Faith

Bruce and Stan show that the New Testament book of James is bursting with no-nonsense help to help you grow in practical ways, such as perceiving God's will, maintaining a proper perspective on wealth and poverty, and demonstrating true wisdom in your speech and actions.

1 & 2 Corinthians: Finding Your Unique Place in God's Plan

This enlightening study explores the apostle Paul's helpful responses to issues that churches continue to face today: maintaining unity in the church, exercising spiritual gifts, and identifying authentic Christian ministry.

Revelation: Unlocking the Mysteries of the End Times

Have you ever read the final chapters of the Scriptures, only to finish with more questions than answers? Bruce and Stan help you understand Revelation's encouraging message and apply it to your life today.

Download a Deeper Experience

Bruce and Stan are part of a faith-based online community called ConversantLife.com. At this website, people engage their faith in entertainment, creative arts, science and technology, global concerns, and other culturally relevant topics. While you're reading this book, or after you have finished reading, go to www.conversantlife.com/101 and use these icons to read and download additional Christianity 101 material from Bruce and Stan.

Resources: Download study guide materials for personal devotions or a small-group Bible study.

Videos: Click on this icon for interviews and video clips on various topics.

Blogs: Read through blogs and articles and comment on them.

Podcasts: Stream ConversantLife.com podcasts and audio clips.

conversant life .com

engage your faith